A
LITTLE
GUIDE
TO
WILD
FLOWERS

This book belongs to

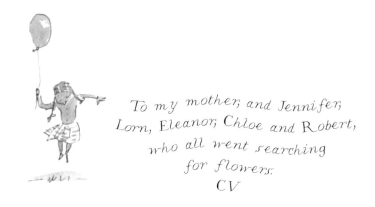

To my mother, and Jennifer,
Lorn, Eleanor, Chloe and Robert,
who all went searching
for flowers.
CV

SC ~ In memoriam
KP

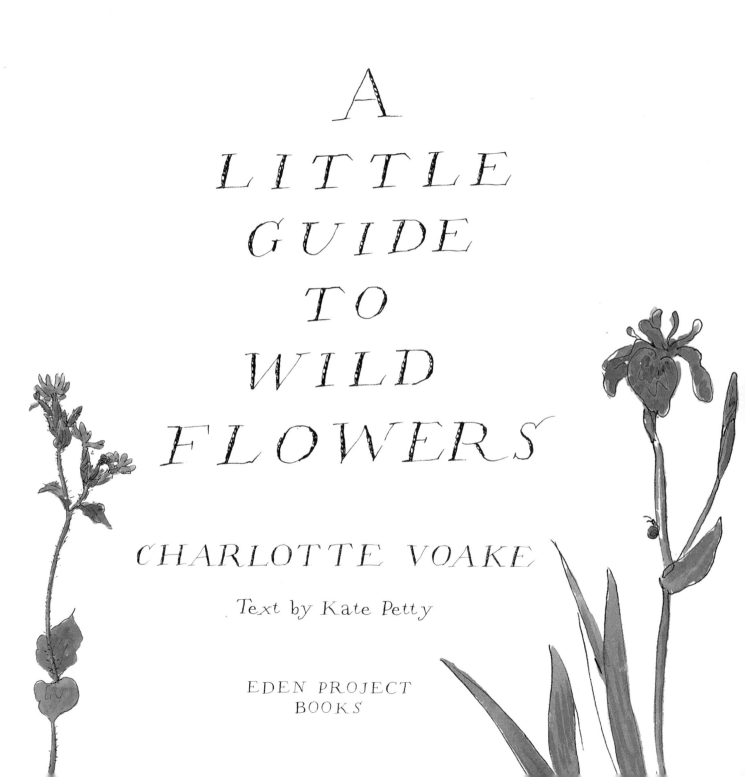

A LITTLE GUIDE TO WILD FLOWERS

CHARLOTTE VOAKE

Text by Kate Petty

EDEN PROJECT
BOOKS

CONTENTS

INTRODUCTION

Discover the names of the wild flowers
that you see every day ~ by the roads, as weeds
in your garden, or between the cracks in the
pavement ~ as well as the ones you'll find in
the countryside or by the sea.

This book groups flowers by colour.
Under each picture is a note of the height
of the plant, where it grows, when it
flowers and its botanical name. These details
will help you to tell similar flowers apart.

See if you can learn the names of fifty different
flowers. There are plenty of extra facts and stories
here to help you remember them.

Don't pick flowers that are growing in the wild.
Look at them closely and leave them there
for the next person to enjoy.
You could even try drawing
them for yourself.

THE SEASONS

Plants will look different
depending on which
season of the
year you see them.

SPRING

Most plants are just putting out
their first shoots. Flowers like
primroses, wild daffodils and
violets start to bloom. Soon yellow
celandines and dandelions can be seen in
the grass verges. Later, bluebells, wild garlic
and wood anemones in the woods show that
summer is on its way.

SUMMER

Early summer is the time when the
roadside banks are full of
campions, cow parsley, stitchwort,
dog daisies, buttercups and clover.
Foxgloves bloom in the woods,
thrift and bladder campions
by the sea.

AUTUMN

As summer passes, you will start to see seedheads and fruits replacing some flowers. Other flowers keep going until the weather gets cold. Look out for bindweed on hedges and fences and Michaelmas daisies by the road.

WINTER

In winter many plants completely disappear as the temperature drops, and everything looks dead. But gorse, with its bright yellow flowers, blooms even in the coldest weather. Watch out for the first leaves of daffodils and bluebells pushing up through the cold ground, and when the tiny white snowdrops appear, spring is not far behind.

LOOKING AT FLOWERS

Petals

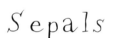

A primrose has five petals.

A daisy has hundreds.

Sepals

Most flowers have a set of little green leaves at the back of the petals called sepals.

Stamens

You can find these in the centre of the flower. They have pollen on them ～ yellow dust.

TYPES OF LEAVES

Several leaves grouped together to make one.

Clover

Small rounded leaves with a slight shine.

Daisy

Large leaves, soft and downy with crinkled wavy edges.

Foxglove

Leaves with uneven, toothed edges.

Dandelion

Long, pointed leaves.

Bluebell

The leaf is as important as the flower when you are trying to identify a plant. Look at the size, the shape and the texture. Often plants with similar flowers have quite different leaves.

LESSER CELANDINE

Spring is on its way when celandines turn the grass verge into a carpet of golden stars and heart~shaped leaves.

10 cm
Woods, hedgerows, banks
Early spring

Ranunculus ficaria
buttercup family

The lesser celandine is no relation of the greater celandine.

CELANDINES COME OUT BEFORE BUTTERCUPS

PRIMROSE

Primrose is the 'prima rosa', the 'first rose'. Smell one if you can ~ the scent is lovely.

20 cm
Roadside and railway banks, woods
Early spring

Primula vulgaris
primrose family

LOOK OUT FOR PRIMROSES UNDER THE HEDGES IN EARLY SPRING

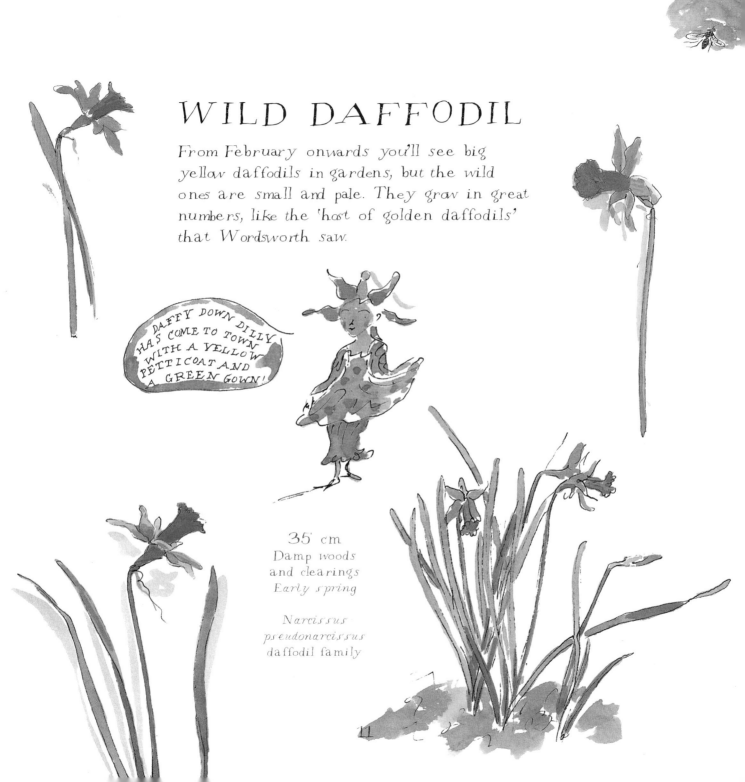

WILD DAFFODIL

From February onwards you'll see big yellow daffodils in gardens, but the wild ones are small and pale. They grow in great numbers, like the 'host of golden daffodils' that Wordsworth saw.

DAFFY DOWN DILLY HAS COME TO TOWN WITH A YELLOW PETTICOAT AND A GREEN GOWN!

35 cm
Damp woods
and clearings
Early spring

*Narcissus
pseudonarcissus*
daffodil family

11

COLTSFOOT

The big woolly leaf of a coltsfoot is the shape of a young pony's hoof. It appears some time after the flower.

Coltsfoot leaves were once used for cough medicine.

COWSLIP

Feel lucky if you come across the sweet~smelling cowslip because it's not very common nowadays.

30 cm
Fields, banks
Spring

Primula veris
primrose family

25 cm
Waste places
Early spring

Tussilago farfara
daisy family

COW-SLYPPE MEANS COW PAT

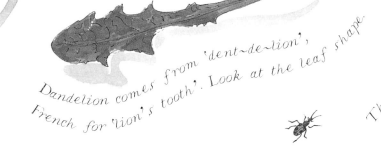

Dandelion comes from 'dent~de~lion', French for 'lion's tooth'. Look at the leaf shape.

The fluffy seedheads are called 'clocks'.

DANDELION

Dandelion flowers open up in the sun like little suns themselves. You can eat the young leaves but watch out ~ another name for dandelion is wet~the~bed.

35 cm
Everywhere
Spring to autumn

Taraxacum officinale
daisy family

THREE PUFFS.
ALL GONE!
IT MUST BE
THREE
O'CLOCK

13

ALEXANDERS

Look out for this tall plant on cliff paths,
the first seaside greenery of the year.
The Romans brought it with
them to eat ~ leaf, stem, root,
buds and all.

1 m
Near sea
Summer

*Smyrnium
olusatrum*
hemlock family

GORSE

There's a saying which goes,
'When gorse is out of blossom,
then kissing's out of fashion'
~ because gorse flowers
all year round! It smells
of coconut.

2 m
Heaths, commons,
cliff paths
All year round

Ulex europaeus
pea family

Gorse's other name, 'Furze', means 'fires', as it burns easily.

The green hairstreak butterfly likes gorse.

PENNYWORT

You might find this unusual~looking
flower growing in rocky crevices
at the seaside. It's also called
navelwort, because the leaves
are round, like little bellies
with bellybuttons.

30 cm
Rock crevices and walls
Summer

Umbilicus rupestris
crassula family

50 cm
Damp places
Summer

Meconopsis
cambrica
poppy
family

WELSH POPPY

You don't need to visit Wales to
see a Welsh poppy. It likes damp,
rocky places in other parts of
the country too.

HEARTSEASE

This is a wild pansy. Sometimes
the petals are white and purple
as well as yellow, which is why
it is also known as *Viola tricolor*.

30 cm
Waste ground, fields
Summer

Viola tricolor
violet family

YELLOW ARCHANGEL

This is a deadnettle, so it won't sting you.
The flowers look a bit like little mouths ~
the botanical name means 'weasel snout'.

60 cm
Shady places
Summer

Galeobdolon luteum
mint family

GREATER CELANDINE

Greater celandine is a member of the poppy
family and no relation to the lesser celandine.
The stem contains a bright orange
sap, which is poisonous.

75 cm
Banks, roadsides
Summer

Chelidonium majus
poppy family

Greater celandine's botanical name means 'swallow'. You see the
flower and the bird during the same summer months.

If your chin shines yellow, you like butter!

BUTTERCUP

This is the meadow buttercup.
Cows and horses won't eat the
bitter plants, but bees and other
insects love the flowers.
If there are plenty,
find out if your
friends like butter.

1 m
Everywhere
All summer

Ranunculus acris
buttercup family

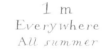

DO YOU LIKE BUTTER?

YES I DO.

55 cm
Marshy places
Spring and
summer

Caltha palustris
buttercup family

18

YELLOW FLAG

This magnificent wild iris is possibly
the original fleur~de~lys, emblem
of kings. Look for it near water
but don't cut yourself on
the sharp leaves.

fleur~de~lys

1~2 m
Near water
Summer

Iris pseudacorus
iris family

KINGCUP or
MARSH MARIGOLD

Both names suit this flower,
but if you try to get too close
to the shiny golden cups you
might end up sinking into the
marsh where it grows. People used
to hang kingcups upside~down
outside their houses as protection
against witches and lightning.

IRIS LEAVES MAKE GOOD BOATS

HERB BENNET
or WOOD AVENS

Herb Bennet means herb
of St Benedict, and this
little flower was once
worn to ward off
evil spirits.

60 cm
Damp and shady places
Summer

Geum urbanum
rose family

The prickly fruit heads are designed to catch on fur and feathers.

LESSER
TREFOIL

Some people think this is the true shamrock
of Ireland. Butterflies and bees
like it for its sweet~
smelling nectar.

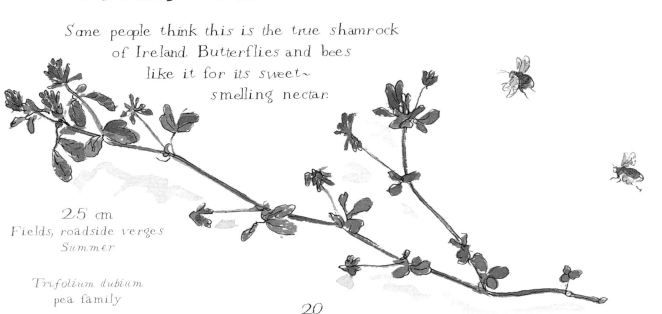

25 cm
Fields, roadside verges
Summer

Trifolium dubium
pea family

20

GROUNDSEL

With its yellow flowers and fluffy seed heads, groundsel looks like tiny dandelions. It flowers and produces seeds almost all year round.

I LIKE A BIT OF GROUNDSEL

ME TOO, MY DEAR

30 cm
Wasteland, footpaths
All year

Senecio vulgaris
daisy family

BIRD'S~FOOT TREFOIL

A very jolly little plant ~ the seed pods are shaped like a bird's foot. Trefoil means 'three leaves'.

30 cm
Grassy places, roadsides
Summer

Lotus corniculatus
pea family

Also known as eggs-and-bacon, cuckoo's stockings, Tom Thumb, lady's slipper, bellies and bums.

21

OILSEED RAPE

This is the crop that paints the fields bright yellow in spring. The seeds are pressed for oil that has all sorts of uses in industry and animal feed as well as in food.

1 m
Roadsides and waste places
Early summer

Brassica napus
wallflower family

THESE ARE ALL FLOWERS YOU CAN SEE FROM A CAR!

SOWTHISTLE

Sometimes known as milk thistle for its milky stems, sowthistle is a very common weed. Rabbits love it!

1 m
Ploughed fields, wasteland
Summer

Sonchus oleraceus
daisy family

22

RAGWORT

Ragwort is a messy-looking plant that is poisonous to grazing animals. It's often covered in the stripy caterpillars of the Cinnabar moth.

TANSY

Smell the feathery leaves ~ tansy was one of the 'bitter herbs' that people ate long ago at Easter time. The flowers look like little buttons. The name tansy comes from the Greek word for immortality, 'athanasia', because the plants were used for packing round corpses awaiting burial.

1 m
Waysides
Late summer

Tanacetum vulgare
daisy family

1 m
Railway banks, roadsides, wasteland
Summer

Senecio jacobaea
daisy family

You can tell ragwort by its ragged leaves.

Bees can't get at the nectar deep in the trumpet-shaped flowers, but long-tongued moths can. They are attracted by the scent on warm summer evenings.

HONEYSUCKLE

Honeysuckle flowers are creamy-white at first, turning yellow later on, and tinged with pink or red. You'll often see honeysuckle in gardens, but it's better still to come across it winding up through the hedgerows in country lanes.

The berries which follow the flowers are poisonous.

2~6 m
Hedgerows
Summer

Lonicera periclymenum
honeysuckle family ~ these are woody plants rather than flowers

24

KIDNEY VETCH

You'll often find these yellow
vetches growing near the sea.
Silky hairs make
them fluffy.

TOADFLAX

Toadflax has the same 'bunny
mouths' as its garden relation,
the snapdragon. Gently squeeze
the flower to make the
orange mouth open
and shut.

50 cm
Grassland,
footpaths
Summer

Linaria vulgaris
figwort family

50 cm
Grassland, footpaths, cliffs
Summer

Anthyllis vulneraria
pea family

CROAK!

SPURGE

There are lots of spurges, all with green, cup-shaped flowers that are as poisonous as they look, and pollinated by flies. This is the 'petty' spurge.

30 cm
Waste places
Summer

Euphorbia peplus
spurge family

STINKING HELLEBORE

The hellebore is related to the Christmas rose. The lower leaves are different from the upper ones.

50 cm
Woods in chalky places
Early spring

Helleborus foetidus
buttercup family

GOOSEGRASS
or CLEAVERS

Goosegrass isn't a grass at all. The little burrs that stick to your clothes are meant to stick to animal fur, so that the seeds can be distributed far and wide.

1 m
Hedges and thickets
Summer

Galium aparine
madder family

STINGING NETTLE

The *sting is in the* hairs. If you 'grasp the nettle' you squash the hairs so they don't sting you. Stinging nettles grow where humans have lived because they like soil that is rich from dung and compost. Young nettle leaves are good to eat if they are cooked.

1 m
Footpaths, hedgerows, clearings
Summer

Urtica dioica
nettle family

Dock leaves soothe a nettle sting.

SNOWDROP

Snowdrops poke up through the snow,
a sign of hope in deep winter.
A whole bank of snowdrops is
a rare but wonderful sight.

20 cm
Thin woods, meadows,
but mostly gardens
Winter

Galanthus nivalis
daffodil family

CHICKWEED

Chickweed grows everywhere and can be seen flowering almost all year round. There are several sorts that all look similar.

40 cm
Fields, gardens, footpaths
All year, but mostly summer

Stellaria media
pink family

SHEPHERD'S PURSE

The seedpods really are shaped like miniature purses. Shepherd's purse, like chickweed, can be found almost anywhere all year round.

30 cm
Fields, gardens, wasteland
All year

Capsella bursa~pastoris
wallflower family

WHITE DEADNETTLE

Here's a nettle that won't sting you! In fact, deadnettles aren't nettles at all but members of the mint family.

40 cm
Footpaths, wasteland, hedgerows, roadsides
All year

Lamium album
mint family

29

Can you see why another name for this flower is Granny's nightcap?

WOOD SORREL

This fragile flower has clover~like leaves that fold up in the rain and taste very sharp if you eat them. The clue is in the botanical names, both of which mean 'acidic'.

30 cm
*Leafy soil,
woodlands
Early spring*

*Oxalis acetosella
oxalis family*

WOOD ANEMONE or WINDFLOWER

The frilly leaves tell you that this is a wood anemone. You'll see lots of them together, flowers nodding in the breeze, turning to protect the pollen from blowing away. The plants disappear completely when spring is over.

30 cm
*Leafy soil,
woodlands
Early spring*

*Anemone nemorosa
buttercup family*

30

The botanical name means 'bear's garlic'.

WOODRUFF or SWEET WOODRUFF

Woodruff flowers are sweet~scented but, once dried, the whole plant has a pleasant smell and can be used for flavouring drinks or putting in the linen drawer.

30 cm
Leafy soil,
chalk woodland
Spring

Galium odoratum
madder family

RAMSONS or WILD GARLIC

If you smell onions in a bluebell wood, ramsons with its starry flowers will be the reason. The big green leaves can be eaten as a garlic substitute.

30 cm
Damp soil,
woodlands
Spring

Allium ursinum
lily family

GREATER STITCHWORT

Stitchwort got its name
because it was used
as a cure for a stitch ~
from running fast.
You can see why
it's also known
as starwort.

50 cm
Roadsides and tall grass
Early summer

Stellaria holostea
pink family

Look for the notched petals.

Caterpillars of the orange~tip butterfly blend in with the pods they eat.

JACK~BY~THE~HEDGE
or GARLIC MUSTARD

Long ago people ate this
common leafy plant all
the time. Today you might
have to pay more than
a pound a bunch for a winter
salad Smelling of garlic and
tasting of mustard, the leaves
have to be picked before
the flowers appear.

90 cm
Damp woods, shady
hedgerows
Early summer

Alliaria petiolata
wallflower family

RIBWORT PLANTAIN

This is the most common plantain, plentiful enough to pick and play shooting games with. That's why some people call them 'soldiers'.

30 cm
Footpaths, lawns, fields
Summer

Plantago lanceolata
plantain family

To shoot a plantain, loop a stem behind the flower head and pull sharply.

20 cm
Grassy banks, woods, hedgerows
Spring

Fragaria vesca
rose family

WILD STRAWBERRY

Here's one you can eat! As spring turns to summer, the flowers turn into small, sweet, red strawberries.

DAISY

A wild flower so common that we take it for granted, but did you know that each flowerhead is actually made up of about 250 tiny flowers? Daisy comes from 'day's eye', because daisies close up at night.

LET'S MAKE A DAISY CHAIN! LEAVE A LONG STEM. MAKE A SLIT HALF WAY DOWN WITH YOUR THUMB NAIL AND THREAD THE NEXT DAISY THROUGH, STALK FIRST.

6 cm
Short grass, lawns, fields
Nearly all year round

Bellis perennis
daisy family

WHITE CLOVER

Good for cows and good for bees! Clover honey is delicious. Clover has three leaves but if you look hard you might find one with four leaves to bring you good luck.

25 cm
Grassy places
Summer

Trifolium repens
pea family

34

COW PARSLEY

This is the flower that dresses green lanes with a froth of white lace in early summer.

1 m
Roadsides, edges of woods
Early summer

Anthriscus sylvestris
hemlock family

PIGNUT

The pignuts are in fact the round roots of this flower that country people used to grub up and eat. It's now illegal to dig for them without permission.

50 cm
Woodland and grassy places
Summer

Conopodium majus
hemlock family

DOG DAISY or OX~EYE DAISY

Also known as a marguerite. This is a big daisy that you often see in great numbers on motorway verges and roundabouts in midsummer.

65 cm
Grassy banks, fields
Summer

Chrysanthemum leucanthemum
daisy family

MEADOW SWEET
or QUEEN OF THE MEADOW

A fluffy, sweetly~scented
flower, with leaves as
soft as rabbits' ears
underneath. Look
for it by streams.

1 m
Wet places
Summer

Filipendula ulmaria
rose family

THE WORD
ASPIRIN COMES
FROM MEADOWSWEET'S
EARLIER BOTANICAL
NAME ~ SPIRAEA
ULMARIA

DROP~
WORT

A smaller relation
of meadowsweet
that grows in dry,
grassy places.
The buds are
tipped with red.

60 cm
Dry grassland, chalk
Summer

Filipendula vulgaris
rose family

36

YARROW

The tiny flowers of a yarrow
flowerhead are sometimes pink as
well as white, but you can tell it by
its herby~smelling, feathery leaves.

60 cm
Meadows, hedges,
roadsides
Summer

Achillea millefolium
daisy family

Millefolium ~ thousand leaves ~ describes the leaf shape.

Yarrow leaves contain a chemical that helps to stop bleeding.

WHITE CAMPION

Look for campions, white and red,
in summer hedgerows.
Sometimes they combine
to make pink ones.

Moths are attracted to the white flowers
at night and pollinate them.

CAMPION IS AN OLD
WORD FOR CHAMPION

80 cm
Roadsides,
hedgerows
Summer

Silene alba
pink family

HAIRY BITTERCRESS

20 cm
Dry, bare ground
and rocky places
Summer

Cardamine hirsuta
wallflower family

You'll see this common
little weed in lots of
dry, waste places,
but it's not as
hairy as it
sounds!

The unopened bud is furled like an umbrella

Trailing stems up to 3 m
Hedges, bushes near streams
Late summer

Calystegia sepium
bindweed family

WHITE BINDWEED
or LARGE BINDWEED

One name for this bindweed, bellbine, describes
its lovely big bell~like flowers, but another,
hedge~strangler, gives a more sinister
picture of its tightly twining tendrils.

BLADDER
CAMPION

If the part below the
petals is puffed up like
a balloon, you've found
a bladder campion

80 cm
Fields, roadsides
Summer

Silene vulgaris
pink family

LADY'S SMOCK
or CUCKOO FLOWER

A tall clump of lady's smock in a marshy meadow can look white from a distance, but close to, the flowers are pale pink or mauve.

70 cm
Wet and marshy places
Early summer

Cardamine pratensis
wallflower family

RAGGED ROBIN

The petals have a torn and tattered look and the flowers feel slightly sticky.

70 cm
Wet and damp places
Early summer

Lychnis flos-cuculi
pink family

YOU CAN SING HEAR ME CUCKOO WHEN THESE FLOWERS ARE IN BLOOM

DOG ROSE
or WILD ROSE

Pretty, single roses of the palest pink are splashed all over great, prickly bushes that are part of hedgerows or stand alone. In autumn the flowers are replaced by orangey-red rosehips, source of rosehip syrup and full of vitamin C.

Bushes 1-2 m
Woods, hedgerows, untended land
Midsummer

Rosa canina
rose family

Midsummer hedgerows are full of flowers.

40

HERB ROBERT

The *wild geranium* can be seen all *year* round. *S*ometimes the flowers are *white*, and the musky~scented leaves *vary* from *bright* green to *brown* and *red*.

RED CAMPION

This is one flower you are almost bound to see in *summer* hedgerows down leafy lanes, protected from the sun.

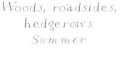

80 cm
Woods, roadsides,
hedgerows
Summer

Silene dioica
pink family

45 cm
Woods, hedgebanks,
walls, gardens
Almost all year

Geranium robertianum
geranium family

41

THRIFT or SEA~PINK

Blue sea, blue sky and pink, thrift~covered cliffs are the glorious colours of a seaside walk in early summer.

30 cm
Seaside, also gardens
Early summer

Armeria maritima
sea~lavender family

10 cm
Salt marshes,
rocky crevices
near the sea
Summer

Spergularia rubra
pink family

SPURREY

The little red sand spurrey plant doesn't mind salty soil so it flowers happily near the sea.

REDSHANK or PERSICARIA

A weed that you'll find everywhere. There are wildly differing explanations for the dark spots on the leaves, such as Christ's blood, or a pinch from the devil!

70 cm
Waste places,
fields, ditches
Summer

Polygonum persicaria
knotgrass family

42

RED CLOVER

Like its white cousin, red clover is good for cows and bees ~ milk and honey. Dried flowerheads were once used as remedies for tummy~aches and sleep problems.

50 cm
Grassy places, fields and lawns
Summer

Trifolium pratense
pea family

FUMITORY

The name comes from the old French 'fume terre' ~ 'smoke of the earth' ~ because the smoky green leaves rise like smoke from disturbed earth.

50 cm
Roadsides, disturbed earth
Summer

Fumaria officinalis
fumitory family

BROAD~LEAVED WILLOWHERB

ROSEBAY WILLOWHERB

This is the more showy member of the willowherb family, the pink flowers often covering demolition sites and burnt ground. It's also known as fireweed. The fluffy white seeds are carried on the wind.

This willowherb has very small pink flowers, one to a stem. You see it everywhere.

60 cm
Woods, hedgerows, roadside, walls
Midsummer

Epilobium montanum
evening primrose family

ONCE RED FLAMES NOW PINK FLOWERS

1.5 m
Wasteland, disturbed ground
Summer

Chamaenerion angustifolium
evening primrose family

RED VALERIAN

Red valerian can be deep pink
or white. Tortoiseshell
butterflies love this
garden flower
that is common
by railways
and roads and
on cliffs.

1.5 m
*Woods, grassland,
amongst other
tall flowers
Summer*

*Centranthus ruber
valerian family*

WOUNDWORT

This is marsh woundwort,
a member of the mint family
like all deadnettles.
Look out for the
spotted flowers.

80 cm
*Wet places
Summer*

*Stachys palustris
mint family*

45

POPPY

The common red poppy ~ or field poppy ~ is one of our biggest and most beautiful wild flowers. The open flower is like red silk, but the crumpled, papery petals inside the buds are very pretty too.

Poppies like disturbed ground, and many appeared on battlefields after the First World War, reminding people of the blood shed by so many soldiers. We wear poppies to remember them.

60 cm
Fields, wasteland, edges of footpaths
Summer

Paparer rhoeas
poppy family

Poppy seeds are used in cakes and bread.

46

MONTBRETIA
or CROCOSMIA

More orange than red, and not a wild flower
at all, but a South African garden
escapee that has taken over many
roadside verges. Look out for it
well into September, blending in
with the autumn colours.

80 cm
Roadsides, banks,
gardens
Late summer

Crocosmia hybrida
iris family

SCARLET
PIMPERNEL

The tiny, bright red flowers take you by surprise
as they trail across a footpath beneath your feet.
They close when rain is on the way, so the
scarlet pimpernel is sometimes known
as 'poor man's weatherglass'.

25 cm
Fields, waste ground,
footpaths
Summer

Anagallis arvensis
primrose family

47

GROUND IVY

This tiny purple flower has
ivy~shaped leaves, but it isn't ivy
at all. Maybe you should call it
by one of its other names, such as
Runaway Jack, Creeping Charlie
or Robin~run~up~the~dyke...

25 m
Woods, hedges, wasteland
Early spring

Glechoma hederacea
mint family

SWEET
VIOLETS
FOR
SALE!

VIOLET

You can sometimes smell the strong perfume
of violets before you spot the little flowers
peeping out from banks and under hedges.
This is the sweet violet, famous
for its scent.

25 cm
Banks, under hedges,
edge of woods
Early spring

Viola odorata
violet family

48

BUSH VETCH

Vetches are members of the pea family.
Bush vetch climbs through hedges and has
beaked dark pods. It is sometimes
known as crow peas.

60 cm
Hedges and woods
Summer

Vicia sepium
pea family

CAW!

IVY-LEAVED TOADFLAX

Look on old walls and steps for trails of tiny purple
flowers turning their faces up towards the light.
When the flowers are over, the fruits turn the
other way so the seeds are buried in the
cracks and crevices.

70 cm
Walls and
stony places
Summer

Cymbalaria muralis
figwort family

FOXGLOVE

The flowers make perfect
mittens for foxes and
thimbles for witches.
The leaves make the
heart medicine, digitalis,
but the whole plant
is poisonous, so it is
best left alone.

1 m
*Woods, hedgerows,
banks
Summer*

*Digitalis
purpurea
figwort
family*

SELF~HEAL

Once the country person's cure for
all ills, self~heal takes its botanical
name from the throat
condition it was
supposed to cure ~
prunella, or quinsy.

20 cm
*Fields, banks,
grass verges
Summer*

*Prunella vulgaris
mint family*

Furry bumblebees are just the right size
to pollinate foxgloves.

COLUMBINE

Columbine means dove ~ look for the dove shape in the petals.

70 cm
Woodland, gardens
Early summer

Aquilegia vulgaris
buttercup family

SCABIOUS

This is field scabious. There are several types, all with tough, long stems. Scabious is an ugly name for a pretty flower. It was used to treat the scabs of the disease scabies.

80 cm
Roadside banks, footpaths, fields
Summer

Knautia arvensis
teasel family

MALLOW

Common mallow is an unmistakable tall plant with lots of big purple flowers that grows by the sides of roads and footpaths.

Another name for Mallow is Rags~and~Tatters.

1.5 m
Footpaths, roadsides, fields, waste ground
Summer

Malva sylvestris
mallow family

TEASEL

Tall teasels look good even
when the flowers are over.
The prickly heads were
used for combing ~
'teasing' ~ the knots
out of sheep's wool.

The soft, fluffy seeds
are called thistledown.

THISTLE

Be careful! Thistle
prickles can draw blood.
The Scotch thistle is the
emblem of Scotland, but this
creeping thistle is
a nuisancy weed.

1 m
Roadsides and fields
Summer

Cirsium arvense
daisy family

MMM
THISTLES!

2 m
Roadsides and fields
Summer

Dipsacus fullonum
teasel family

KNAPWEED
or HARD~HEAD

Knapweed looks like a thistle,
but it *isn't* prickly, even
though it has a very tough
stalk. The picture shows
lesser knapweed The leaves
of greater knapweed are
more feathery.

50 cm
Waysides
Summer

Centaurea nigra
daisy family

People once used knapweed
to cure cuts and bruises.

The botanical name for these flowers
refers to the wise centaur Chiron
of Greek myth.

53

Comfrey flowers can be purple, white or cream.

WOODY NIGHTSHADE

This is a common member of the potato family and *not* to be confused with deadly nightshade, which has all~purple flowers and black, deadly poisonous berries. The red berries of woody nightshade shouldn't be eaten either.

1.75 m
Hedges, banks, woodland
Summer

Solanum dulcamara
potato family

COMFREY

A very leafy plant when growing, and rough to the touch. Also called knitbone, comfrey root was scraped into a gel and used to set broken bones in the same way as a plaster cast is used today.

1 m
Damp places
Summer

Symphytum officinale
borage family

HEATHER

Springy underfoot, heather turns huge areas of moorland and heath purple in early autumn. Sprigs of white heather are worn for good luck.

60 cm
Heaths, moors, pinewoods
Autumn

Calluna vulgaris
heather family

Michaelmas is September 29th.

MICHAELMAS DAISY

Here's another flower that has escaped from gardens to appear all over railway embankments and roadside verges in autumn. Butterflies love to bask in the sun on Michaelmas daisies.

1.5 m
Roadsides, railway embankments, gardens
Autumn

Aster novi~belgii
daisy family

BLUEBELL

Bluebells wash through woods and hedgerows in a tide of blue in May. It's worth going out of your way to see a bluebell wood in flower.

Bluebells are wild hyacinths and share their beautiful scent.

30 cm
Woodlands, hedgerows, under trees
Spring

Endymion non scriptus
lily family

Myosotis means mouse~ear ~ look at the leaf shape.

FORGET~ ME~NOT

We don't know why these pretty blue and pink flowers are called forget~me~nots, but it's an unforgettable name! Perhaps it's because they are little. Look for wild ones by streams and rivers.

45 cm
Wet places, gardens
Early summer

Myosotis
borage family

SPEEDWELL

Tiny speedwell flowers don't last long. They peep up from the grass like bright little eyes. This is germander speedwell ~ you can see why it's known as bird's~ eye speedwell in some places.

Germander means 'small oak' and describes the leaf shape.

35 cm
Hedgerows, grassland and woods
Early summer

Veronica chamaedrys
figwort family

ALKANET

This is evergreen alkanet, a leafy garden escapee that can fill hedgerows and banks. The leaves are rough and hairy.

80 cm
Hedgerows, gardens
Early summer

Pentaglottis sempervirens
borage family

CORNFLOWER

Once upon a time,
golden cornfields
were bejewelled
with red poppies
and blue cornflowers.
Today you're
more likely to find
cornflowers in gardens.
Look out, too, for
the bigger, tougher
perennial cornflower.

80 cm
Cornfields,
waste ground
Summer

Centaurea cyanus
daisy family

MILKWORT

The little milkwort plant
makes the pasture richer
for cows ~ the botanical
name means 'much milk'.
Sometimes the flowers
are blue, pink and white
all on one stem.

20 cm
Grassy places
Summer

Polygala vulgaris
milkwort
family

HAREBELL
or SCOTTISH BLUEBELL

When growing, the delicate, papery harebell flowers hang downwards. The slightest breeze would make them tinkle if they were real bells.

40 cm
Grassy places, coast paths
Summer

Jasione montana
bellflower family

30 cm
Meadows, rocky and grassy places
Late summer

Campanula rotundifolia
bellflower family

SHEEP'S BIT

This flower looks like scabious but belongs to a different family. It grows in dry, grassy places where sheep like to graze. 'Bit' means 'bite'.

BAA!

Baa!

INDEX

Old Man's Beard in autumn.

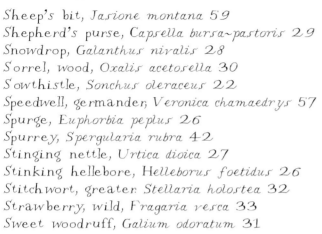

TICK LIST

Tick off the flowers as you find them.

- [ ] Alexanders
- [ ] Alkanet
- [ ] Bird's~foot trefoil
- [ ] Bladder campion
- [ ] Bluebell
- [ ] Broad~leaved willowherb
- [ ] Bush vetch
- [ ] Buttercup
- [ ] Chickweed
- [ ] Coltsfoot
- [ ] Columbine
- [ ] Comfrey
- [ ] Cornflower
- [ ] Cow parsley
- [ ] Cowslip
- [ ] Daisy
- [ ] Dandelion
- [ ] Dog daisy
- [ ] Dog rose
- [ ] Dropwort
- [ ] Forget~me~not
- [ ] Foxglove
- [ ] Fumitory
- [ ] Goosegrass
- [ ] Gorse
- [ ] Greater celandine
- [ ] Greater stitchwort
- [ ] Ground ivy
- [ ] Groundsel
- [ ] Hairy bittercress
- [ ] Harebell
- [ ] Heartsease

- [ ] Heather
- [ ] Herb bennet
- [ ] Herb robert
- [ ] Honeysuckle
- [ ] Ivy~leaved toadflax
- [ ] Jack~by~the~hedge
- [ ] Kidney vetch
- [ ] Kingcup
- [ ] Knapweed
- [ ] Lady's smock
- [ ] Lesser celandine
- [ ] Lesser trefoil
- [ ] Mallow
- [ ] Meadowsweet
- [ ] Michaelmas daisy
- [ ] Milkwort
- [ ] Montbretia
- [ ] Oilseed rape
- [ ] Pennywort
- [ ] Pignut
- [ ] Poppy
- [ ] Primrose
- [ ] Ragged robin
- [ ] Ragwort
- [ ] Ramsons
- [ ] Red campion
- [ ] Red clover
- [ ] Redshank
- [ ] Red valerian
- [ ] Ribwort plantain
- [ ] Rosebay willowherb
- [ ] Scabious
- [ ] Scarlet pimpernel

- [ ] Self~heal
- [ ] Sheep's bit
- [ ] Shepherd's purse
- [ ] Snowdrop
- [ ] Sowthistle
- [ ] Speedwell
- [ ] Spurge
- [ ] Spurrey
- [ ] Stinging nettle
- [ ] Stinking hellebore
- [ ] Tansy
- [ ] Teasel
- [ ] Thistle
- [ ] Thrift
- [ ] Toadflax
- [ ] Violet
- [ ] Welsh poppy
- [ ] White bindweed
- [ ] White campion
- [ ] White clover
- [ ] White deadnettle
- [ ] Wild daffodil
- [ ] Wild strawberry
- [ ] Wood anemone
- [ ] Woodruff
- [ ] Wood sorrel
- [ ] Woody nightshade
- [ ] Woundwort
- [ ] Yarrow
- [ ] Yellow archangel
- [ ] Yellow flag

The Eden Project brings plants and people together.
It *is* dedicated to developing a greater understanding
of our shared global garden; encouraging us to
respect plants ～ and to protect them.

MY WILD~FLOWER SCRAPBOOK

These are your own pages for keeping a record of the
wild flowers you see and the places in which you find them.

This book will help you to identify the flowers that you find,
perhaps on holiday or just at home throughout the year. You can use
the following pages to list them, draw or paint them, or even stick in
photos, but ONLY pick and press flowers if they grow in your own garden.
The headings are suggestions only: use the space as you wish and
let your imagination run wild. Make sure you date all your
entries ~ this could be a useful document one day!

Enjoy mixing your colours to match the petals and
leaves exactly and don't forget to include some of the
insects you see on the flowers, such as bees, ladybirds
and butterflies ~ even aphids.

This is your space. Fill it with flowers!

PRIMROSE April 5th: There were lots of these at the bottom of the garden.

BLUEBEL

SPRING WILD FLOWERS

VIOLET April 12th: By the steps at school. The violets had a beautiful scent.

HAIRY BITTERCRESS April 19

April 14th: In the woods. I only saw one or two of these. Soon there will be loads.

DAISY April 15th: All over the garden. I nearly forgot to include this!

By the garden wall. This looked exactly like the picture in the book!

SUMMER WILD FLOWERS

BUSH VETCH July 5th: In the hedge. This was a lovely purple colour.

SCARLET PIMPERNEL July 5th.

few bluebells.

COW PARSLEY June 1st: All along the roadside.

DOG ROSE July 4th: In the hedgerows. This is almost my favourite flower.

On the path going into the wood. These were open and the sun was shining.

MONTBRETIA September 1st: All along the roadside. We saw these as we

AUTUMN WILD
FLOWERS AND SEEDS

HAREBELL September 4th: In Scotland on holiday. We saw a few harebells by the path when we went walking.

HEATHER

eft home to go up north.

MICHAELMAS DAISY September 8th: On the railway banks. The banks were covered in these.

September 10th: In Scotland on holiday. Big patches of heather looked completely purple.

WINTER WILD
FLOWERS AND BERRIES

OLD MAN'S BEARD November 29th: In the hedgerow. Mu

SNOWDROP February 5th: Under the cherry tree in the garden. I saw these for the first time today.

ALEXANDERS Feb 7th: On the cliff path. I always wonder

said lots of old man's beard means a cold winter ahead. It's called wild clematis.

CELANDINE Feb 7th: Granny's garden. Quite a few of these are already flowering.

DAISY Feb 7th: Granny's garden. Granny's lawn has quite a few early daisies like this.

what these were when we went to Granny's house by the sea and now I know!

THRIFT

WILD FLOWERS
ON HOLIDAY

FUMITORY

CROAK.

We went to Wales for Whit week and saw all these
growing near the sea. This was the first time I'd seen fumitory.

TOADFLAX

KIDNEY VETCH

SPURREY

WORDS ABOUT
WILD FLOWERS

...erge into a carpet of golden stars.

CELANDINES COME OUT BEFORE BUTTERCUPS

FOXGLOVE The flowers make perfect mittens for foxes and thimbles for witches.

SPEEDWELL They peep up from the grass like bright little eyes.

HONEYSUCKLE July 3rd: I love the smell of honeysuckle on warm summer evenings.

FAVOURITE
WILD FLOWERS

MEADOWSWEET August 9th: One of my favourites, because the leaves are as soft as rabbits' ears.

COLUMBINE June 18th: I love the dove~shaped petals.

DAISY March 30th: Me and my sister made pretty daisy~chain crowns.

TOADFLAX July 15th: I like squeezing the flower to make the orange mouth open and shut.

CORNFLOWER June 29th: Cornflowers are beautiful and blue is my favourite colour!

A LITTLE GUIDE TO WILD FLOWERS
AN EDEN PROJECT BOOK 978 1 903 91911 8

Published in Great Britain by Eden Project Books,
an imprint of Transworld Publishers

This edition published 2007

3 5 7 9 10 8 6 4 2

Text copyright © Kate Petty, 2004
Illustrations copyright © Charlotte Voake, 2004

Plant Consultant: Sue Minter (Head of Living Collections, Eden Project)

Designed by Ness Wood

Set in TW Wildflowers

TRANSWORLD PUBLISHERS
61–63 Uxbridge Rd, London W5 5SA
A division of The Random House Group Ltd

Addresses for companies within The Random House Group Limited
can be found at:www.randomhouse.co.uk/offices.htm

THE RANDOM HOUSE GROUP Limited Reg. No. 954009

www.**kids**at**randomhouse**.co.uk
www.edenproject.com

A CIP catalogue record for this book is available from the British Library.

Printed and bound in Singapore